becoming *myself*

8-session study guide

stasi eldredge

New York Times bestselling coauthor
of *Captivating*

becoming *myself*

*embracing God's
dream of you*

8-session study guide

David C Cook®
transforming lives together

BECOMING MYSELF STUDY GUIDE
Published by David C Cook
4050 Lee Vance View
Colorado Springs, CO 80918 U.S.A.

David C Cook Distribution Canada
55 Woodslee Avenue, Paris, Ontario, Canada N3L 3E5

David C Cook U.K., Kingsway Communications
Eastbourne, East Sussex BN23 6NT, England

The graphic circle C logo is a registered trademark of David C Cook.

The website addresses recommended throughout this book are offered as a
resource to you. These websites are not intended in any way to be or imply an
endorsement on the part of David C Cook, nor do we vouch for their content.

LCCN 2013940874
ISBN 978-0-7814-0955-1
eISBN 978-0-7814-1090-8

© 2013 Stasi Eldredge
Published in association with Yates & Yates, www.yates2.com.

The Team: Don Pape, Karen Lee-Thorp, Nick Lee, Caitlyn Carlson, Karen Athen
Cover Design: Amy Konyndyk

Printed in the United States of America
First Edition 2013

2 3 4 5 6 7 8 9 10

012414

contents

introduction

congratulations and welcome!

Congratulations on your decision to pursue God's vision of who you are to become, and welcome to a truly wonderful journey. It's a journey you've been on your whole life, but now—with intention—you're focusing on it. That means a season of movement, growth, and healing is in store for you. And that is so good!

We are all on the journey of becoming our true selves. Each of our journeys is as unique as our fingerprints. Yet we all have fingerprints just as we all have journeys, so though we are different, there is much that we share. I have learned so much from women who have gone before me—women I have never met and women I live close to. I've learned from their journeys, their insights, their struggles, their victories, and their shared experiences. It is my hope that what I offer here from my own journey will help to shed light on yours. If you are doing this study in a group, then may you learn from and encourage one another as you press on in your own becoming!

This journey of becoming myself, my true self, has taken me up steep paths and down rocky ravines. It can be arduous. A light beckons from around the corner, and in the nick of time I am invited to sit and rest awhile. Take stock. Look back and see how far I've come before once again moving forward.

Some of the time I travel alone, following the signposts left by witnesses who preceded me and the voice of the One who calls me up and on.

Sometimes I travel with others, enjoying their companionship and sharing the experience of pilgrimage. At times, I simply pass a fellow sojourner who offers me a cup of cold water, mercy in a glass, strength for the journey. There are dangerous paths ahead, but there are beautiful pastures as well. And all is unknown terrain as I continue on this road that ultimately leads me Home, where I have been expected, will be celebrated, and once there, will be finally, fully myself.

You see, I want life. I want joy. I want beauty and connection and meaning and the freedom to become the full expression of who God created me to be. I want to live from a heart come alive and shake the dust of useless regret from my soul. I have tasted the goodness of God, and it has awakened my hunger for more. I believe more is available. I believe that the things I want are good and worth pursuing and something that we share. I want to know who I truly am and live unto that. I want to become myself. Fully. Completely. Unashamed and free. And clearly, *so do you.*

But let it be known right from the start that being finally, fully myself is not the ultimate goal. Yes, I long to be true. I want to be a woman who offers others only what is best and encourages them along on their journey Home. But the true treasure is the fact that becoming fully myself means becoming fully his, being completely transformed into the image of Christ. Not losing myself but being utterly found and made wholly, perfectly complete. On that day, I will no longer see dimly as in a glass, but I will see face-to-face the One for whom my every heartbeat yearns. The truth is, I cannot see Jesus fully and clearly until I am myself full and clear.

The marvelous news is that it is God *in us* who is accomplishing this miracle, but our transformation requires our active participation. We have to be awake. We need to be increasingly aware. And we have to want it.

I want it. And since you have chosen to pick up this study guide, I know you want it too. Well, then. Come, Jesus. Help us. Guide us. Let the next season of a deeper transformation begin.

how this study guide works

This guide breaks up the fourteen chapters of *Becoming Myself* into eight sessions. Two of the sessions cover only one chapter each; the other six sessions cover two chapters each. I suggest that you read the entire book through before going back and doing the work in the study guide. That way, you will be somewhat familiar with what is coming. This is particularly true if you are facilitating a discussion of this study!

Whether or not you have read the book through before beginning, read the chapter(s) before you turn your attention to the corresponding study guide session. The guide is not broken into different days or sections, so you are welcome to go at your own pace. If you have an hour, you may end up doing the whole session. If you have ten minutes a day, then simply do what you can in that time.

This study guide invites you to take a deeper look at your life and to continually invite Jesus into the areas that surface. There will be sessions where it would be beneficial to do some journaling in a separate notebook or journal. My hope is that much is stirred in your heart as you read, ponder, and write. To that end, you will want to set apart enough time to do this good work. Some topics may not be easy. Some you may breeze through.

Either way, it is always wise to pray before you begin. Invite the Holy Spirit to guide you and to guard your time. You know how it works: you begin to pray about something, and the phone rings, you smell smoke, or your memory jogs about a thousand other important things you have forgotten. Pray for God to protect your time from distractions. Unplug your phone. Lock the bedroom door. Try to set apart fifteen to thirty minutes to spend on this study each day. It will be worth it. You are worth it.

Some of the sessions will take you longer than others. Truthfully, the more you put into it, the more you will get out. Still, you don't want to rush it, so feel free to take more than one week to do a session! On the other hand, I know that there are seasons when time is not as plentiful as we'd like. To help you—particularly if you are doing this in a group—I've used a leaf to designate key questions that you do not want to miss.

If you are using the companion DVD series, you will follow the same pattern. Read the book. Do the study guide session on your own. Gather with your group to watch the DVD session. Discuss with your group. Ta-da!

May your time, your life, your becoming be blessed!

does anyone really change?

Before you begin responding to the questions in this session, please read chapter 1 in the book *Becoming Myself*.

It's wise to begin each new day and certainly each new work with prayer. So before you dive into the study, please pray! Invite the Holy Spirit to guide you. I like to begin each day—even before I get out of bed—with a simple prayer: *"Jesus, I consecrate my life to you."* I am a woman who happily admits that I need all the help I can get!

So to start:

Jesus, I consecrate myself to you, this day to you, and this study to you. I pray for your guidance and your help. Please fill this time. Quicken my heart and my mind in response to the nudges of your Spirit. I give you permission to take me wherever you want me to go. I am yours. At least, I want to be yours. More and more. In Jesus's Name. Amen.

There. That was good. Now, do you have some time and space for this? Are you sitting at a red light, trying to find a few moments to fit this in, or do you have some room? If you're home, can you unplug or turn off your phone?

Your relationship with Christ, your heart, your becoming yourself is worth time, space, effort, and attention. Breathe deeply. Okay. Ready? Let's begin.

 1. What was stirred in you as you read this first chapter? Hope? Resignation? Passion? Nothing? Take a few moments to check in with your own heart. What has been your response to the thoughts presented?

 2. As you look back at your life, what are some areas you have grown in? (For example, maybe you're less afraid to meet new people, able to kill spiders, less controlling of others …)

 3. You are most likely quite aware of the places in your life that you would like to be different. There are places you long to grow in and areas where you may feel bound to fail over and over again. What are those?

4. I wrote, "Many women feel like a failure as a woman. I know that oftentimes I do. A failure as a human being, really. It has affected just about everything I have done and everything I have been kept from doing" (*Becoming Myself,*

page 14). Is this true for you? And if so, does it relate to the areas you long to change or to something else?

5. Can you remember a time when you were ashamed of who you were and of not being who you wanted to be? If so, what happened?

Invite Jesus into that memory. Just a simple prayer like this is really good: *"Please, Jesus, come into this memory. Come into this place in my heart and minister to me here."*

 6. Have you ever used shame to motivate yourself? Are you still using it? How? (By *shame*, I am referring to an inner dialogue in which you berate yourself for not being or doing what you consider to be the right thing.)

 7. How has shame worked out for you as a motivator? How is it working now?

8. What about discipline? Have you created lists for yourself regarding the ways you want to be living? Are you able to follow through with those lists? In what areas of your life is that more challenging for you?

A key truth in chapter 1 is this:

> The very fact that we long for the change we do is a sign that *we are meant to have it*. Our very dissatisfaction with our weaknesses and struggles points to the reality that continuing to live in them is not our destiny. (*Becoming Myself*, page 15)

9. As you consider the possibility that this really is true, what does it evoke in your heart?

10. Near the end of chapter 1, I ask you to consider the possibility that becoming your truer self is less about your own effort and more about the process of allowing God to restore you. Do you think that is true? And if it's true, how does that make you feel? (Hopeful? Irritated that he seems to be taking so long? What?)

11. In what areas in your life would you love to experience God's deeper restoration of you?

Turning our attention to areas that we would like to change or grow in can often leave us feeling like a failure. That is why it is vitally important that in the same moments of acknowledging our desire for change, we also need to acknowledge this foundational truth: God loves you. Right here. Right now.

I wrote, "God is not going to love me any more or any differently when and if I finally lose this weight and become free from the stranglehold of food. Jesus's love for me, my Father's love for me, never changes. Yeah, okay, fellowship may be strained at times, but his heart toward me does not change. He is passionately in love with me. Even better, I think he likes me. And by the way, he's got a pretty huge thing for you, too. Yes, you" (*Becoming Myself*, page 20).

 12. In the light of God's love, write out your prayer, asking Jesus to come and help you to rest in his love for you and also to bring about the change, the *unveiling*, that you long for. Thank him, by faith, that he is going to do just that.

Let's pray together:

Dear God, you know my story. You know my desires, and you know the places where I have begun to give up hope. Would you please come for me, Jesus? Would you please breathe life and hope into the places of my heart that need to be revived? I pray for your eyes on my life. I pray for the grace to believe more deeply that you love me completely right now, even before I have gained the victory and freedom I long for.

Jesus, I invite you to continue to reshape the way I feel about myself. Holy Spirit, fill me this day and awaken me more deeply to you. I want to let go of shame. I want to let go of striving. But I'm not sure how that intertwines with still trying. I want to cooperate with you. And I want to be free and true. Please unveil the truest me. I need your help. Thank you that you are restoring me, Jesus. I look to you. In Jesus's Name. Amen.

Yesterday morning, as I went for my daily walk/prayer time, the silliest thought went through my head. Thinking of the schedule for the many months ahead and what will be required, I actually said to myself, "If I were me, I'd hire a personal trainer." Hilarious, right? If I were me? *Hmmmm. Guess what, girlfriend—you are you.* I let my thoughts run a little rampant. Looking at my life from a safe distance, I asked myself, "What else would you do, if you were you?" Turns out there's a lot I would do.

It was an interesting exercise. What would I do if I were me but didn't have the responsibility to actually do the work? (I've always thought I could do a great job running other people's lives. Just not so great with my own.) But what would I do with my own life ... really? What would you do with yours?

Who is the woman you want to become? What is she like? Ask God to begin to breathe hope into your heart that you can actually become her.

> By faith, we turn to him. By faith, we choose to believe that
> he hears our prayer. By faith, we believe he is good and is
> for us. By faith, we trust that though we may not see it or
> feel it, God is at work in us and for us. Because he says he is.
> (*Becoming Myself*, page 24)

looking back with mercy/ the landscape of our lives

Before you begin responding to the questions in this session,
please read chapters 2 and 3 in the book *Becoming Myself.*

You know that saying, "Can't see the forest for the trees"? It means that when you are very near to something, you are unable to see it clearly. Being in close proximity to anything—a situation, a relationship, or your own childhood—can hinder your ability to perceive it correctly. That's another reason why I love asking God how he sees things. The Scriptures say that his thoughts and ways are as far above our own as the heavens are higher than the earth (Isa. 55:8–9).

If anyone sees and understands things well, it's God. His view on our life is clear. His understanding of our history is perfect. He looks at our life and does not become exasperated as we might. God's mercy is new every morning (Lam. 3:22–23). He is rich in mercy, abounding in love (Eph. 2:4). We can ask for his view on our life and know that we don't need to brace ourselves for bearing the weight of eternal disappointment. His view is different from ours. We must ask for his eyes on our life. He is merciful to us. We can be merciful too.

Do you remember much about your childhood? What were you like? What did *you* like? What games did you enjoy? Were *you* enjoyed? Just take a few minutes here and ask God to help you remember. What was your childhood like? What do you remember even now? What did you love, dream of, play, feel, believe? Invite Jesus into your memory and into your perception of your youth.

Let's pray.

Dear God, please prepare my heart to remember my childhood. I pray for the grace to remember honestly and the gift to see my life, to see myself, through your eyes. Holy Spirit, come into all my memories. Sanctify my memory. I need you. Come and fill this time. I consecrate it and myself to you. In Jesus's Name. Amen.

shaped by our childhood

 1. How would you describe the soundtrack of your childhood? What sounds do you remember?

 2. What were you like as a young girl? Take a few moments and remember. Describe yourself as a little girl. (Pretty, lively, lonely, scared …)

 3. What is one of your favorite childhood memories?

It's important to remember. But it's also very important to remember *honestly*.

My childhood was not idyllic. Since no one's was, I'm guessing it's a pretty safe bet yours wasn't either. But a deeper understanding of our stories leads to a deeper understanding of ourselves—who we are and who God has made us to be. Yes, there is sorrow there, but there is glory, too.

> *Memory makes it possible for us both to bless the past, even those parts*
> *of it that we have always felt cursed by, and also to be blessed by it.*
> —Frederick Buechner, *Telling Secrets*

The first ten years of a person's life pass all too quickly, but the effect of those years colors the rest of our life. Whether mostly good or mostly awful, most women's childhoods are a mixture of both. These formative years are the foundation of the women we are today.

 4. Is it a new thought for you that your current struggles are rooted in your past? What are your current struggles?

5. When and where did your current struggles begin? Take a few minutes and ask God to help you remember.

6. Are there any people from your childhood whose impact on you was negative, people you need to forgive? Including you? Who are they? For what do they need forgiveness? As much as you are able, in this moment, spend time in prayer and ask God for the grace to forgive them and release them to him.

Part of our healing comes with forgiveness (of ourselves and others), and part of it comes with repentance. But first, we have to begin with how God sees us. How he sees *you*. Do you know?

7. Read Romans 8:38-39. How would you restate this in your own words?

8. Read Romans 8:1. According to this verse, how much condemnation is valid over your life? Why does that matter?

9. Read 2 Corinthians 5:21. What does your Father see when he looks at you?

10. Read Hebrews 13:5. Are you now or will you ever be alone? How does thinking about that affect you? Do you take it in or push it away?

11. From the Scripture passages you've just looked at, how would you summarize the way God sees you?

12. We've pretty well established that I am a hungry woman. Since you are alive, I know that you are hungry too. Are you aware of your inner thirst or hunger? What do you want more of?

13. Take a moment now and pray, inviting Jesus into that hunger. Write out your prayer.

14. How has what you have struggled with drawn you to Jesus? How has it shaped you?

> In my anguish I cried to the LORD,
>   and he answered by setting me free.
>   (Ps. 118:5 NIV 1984)

Okay. I said it's good to remember our past and to remember honestly. Though there is pain in those memories, there is also goodness that some of us have not yet had the eyes to see. Why not ask God to bring to mind gifts from our past that we may not have yet recognized?

15. Ask Jesus to reveal to you places in your past where he was loving you, protecting you, and wooing you to himself. *Were you there, God? Where? How?*

Let God begin to rewrite your story. Invite him to show you your past through his eyes. Ask him to surface good memories you have forgotten. He would love to do it. There is healing to be had there. There is a replacing of regret with mercy.

Our pasts have helped shape us into the women we are today. Other forces are also at work both internally and externally.

the wonder of hormones

 16. Think about the four seasons of a woman's life: preadolescence, menses, perimenopause, and menopause. Which season are you in? If you are in menses, the season of life when you have a period, which week are you in: week 1 (estrogen is released, energy and mood are highest), week 2 (which ends with ovulation), week 3 (estrogen and progesterone are dropping, mood may fall too), or week 4 (period begins)?

17. How are your hormones affecting you?

How crazy would it be to bless your hormones? I'm thinking that the crazier it seems, the better it would be. Our hormones are a gift to us, though one we may not yet have peace with, manage well, or bless. So let's go ahead and bless them!

I bless my body. I thank you, God, for making me a woman. I accept my body and my femininity as a gift. I bless every part of me, perfect or flawed, and these hormones inside me as well. I consecrate my feminine body to the Lord Jesus Christ; I consecrate my hormones to him.

Jesus, come and bring grace and healing here. Speak peace to the storm within me just as you calmed the sea. Come and bless my femininity, and teach me to understand how you have made me and how to live gracefully with the rhythms of my body. Amen.

And now we make a sharp left turn from blessing our femininity to exploring how it has been assaulted. This may be difficult, but stay with me. It's very important.

the hatred of women

> *misogyny:* A hatred of women. From Greek *misein* "to hate" + *gynē* "woman."[1]

18. What rose up in you when you read about the external landscape of your life?

 19. Where in the story of your life have you experienced misogyny?

 20. What do you believe Jesus feels about women? Why?

21. What is the source of hatred against women?

For our struggle is not against flesh and blood, but against the rulers, against the authorities, against the powers of this dark world and against the spiritual forces of evil in the heavenly realms. (Eph. 6:12)

 22. Spend a few minutes in prayer asking God to show you where the Enemy has hurt you or had a heyday in your life. (Did you think it was you or God who was to blame?) Where and when?

 23. What rose up in your heart as you read the last portion of chapter 3 regarding the important role women are meant to play?

 24. Time to pray. We need to invite Jesus into every area of our lives. We need to repent where we need to repent and to obey James's command to submit to God and resist the Devil (James 4:7). Write out your prayer.

Dearest Lord Jesus, I come before you now in humility, seeking your strength and wisdom. Please shed your light on my world, my life, and my body. I do not

want to be ignorant of the Devil's schemes nor blame you or anyone else for what he is doing.

I choose again to bless my body and to bless the fact that I am a woman. Jesus, please reveal to me where the Enemy has hurt me and kept me from living, loving, and offering in the ways I am meant to. I reject every lie of the Enemy.

I submit to you, God, as my Lord, and I resist the lies of Satan. In the Name of Jesus, I command the Enemy to flee from me and from my domain. Jesus, you reign, and you reign in me. I choose to believe the truth: you are God, you love me, and you have given me every spiritual weapon to defeat the schemes of the Enemy. I choose to love. I choose you. I choose to offer my unique feminine strength to my world. In Jesus's beautiful Name, I pray. Amen.

The fruit, dear one, is LIFE! For you. For many.

more to think about

"The degree to which you can tell your story is the degree to which you can heal." A friend spoke these words to me as he relayed the story of a young man who works with women rescued from sex trafficking. His words caught me. More, they stopped me. Because it's actually true. The degree to which you can tell your story is the degree to which you are no longer bound by shame.

Now, I am not suggesting that we tell everyone we know the intimate details of our lives. Our personal histories are marked by joy and sorrow and are holy ground. But there need to be one or two people with whom you are able to share your life's story. Perhaps a counselor. Perhaps your spouse. Perhaps a trusted friend.

Pray and ask God to provide this person to you and to prepare your heart to share. As a preparation, maybe you could spend time simply before God and his eyes of grace. Tell him your story. Tell him your sorrows. Ask him to comfort and heal you. Tell him your sins and your failures. Ask him to forgive you.

The story of your life is one worth telling. It is certainly one worth hearing, learning from, honoring, and paying close attention to.

Suggested Music: "You Know Me" by Bethel Music, featuring Steffany Frizzell
Suggested Reading: Lorraine Pintus, *Jump Off the Hormone Swing*; Neil T. Anderson, *The Bondage Breaker*

our mothers, ourselves

Before you begin responding to the questions in this session,
please read chapters 4 and 5 in the book *Becoming Myself.*

Welcome back. Since you've made it to session 3, I know you are a brave woman. You are also a woman who is serious about pursuing her own healing in order to be able to live, love, and offer as she is meant to.

I am keenly aware that for many women, these two chapters about our mothers can be difficult. If we are mothers ourselves, part of the difficulty comes from our awareness of how we have failed our own children. And for every woman, the larger difficulty comes from the fact that our relationship with our mother is fraught with many emotions. It is sacred ground. So as always, we want to begin with prayer.

Jesus, I need your mercy, your courage, and your boundless grace. I consecrate my life to you again right now. I consecrate my memory, my hopes, my longings, and my desires. I pray you would guide me as I look back. I ask that you hold me close to your heart as together we remember. Mother me, Lord. And yes, I bless my earthly mother right now with more of you, Jesus. I also ask that you help me to mother those in my life whom you have entrusted to me. But I need you to come for me in my own need for mothering. I pray you bring to me all the healing that I so deeply need. I love you, God. I need you. Please come. Thank you that you will and you are. In Jesus's beautiful Name. Amen.

The relationship between mothers and daughters is a deep one. It is foundational. Our mothers affected us *profoundly.* They have shaped us perhaps more than we realize or care to admit. We want to spend some time looking at our relationship with our mothers now and how our mothers have made their imprint on our deepest selves.

We will do that "looking" from a position of humility. We want to honor our mothers. The command to honor your father and your mother is found several times in Scripture. It is the only command with a promise attached: "Honor your father and your mother, so that you may live long in the land the LORD your God is giving you" (Ex. 20:12). Your land may be land, or it may be a calling, a business, a relationship, a ministry. Your land is your territory, your domain.

Too often we have diminished our mothers, both who they are and what they've done. We don't want to do that but rather respect the weighty role they have played in our lives.

 1. Using only adjectives, describe your relationship with your mother.

 2. What was your birth mother's life like while you were in the womb? (If you don't know, what do you think it was like?)

3. Do you think you got enough nourishment while you were being formed in secret (Ps. 139:15) in the womb? In what ways did you or didn't you?

4. Have you ever been told the story of your arrival? To the best of your knowledge, what is it?

 5. In your childhood, did you receive the nourishment you needed in terms of food, medicine, healthy touch, and positive attention? What do you remember?

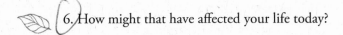 6. How might that have affected your life today?

7. As a teenager, did you receive initiation into womanhood? (Who taught you how to use feminine products? Care for your skin? Fix your hair? Dress in a way flattering to your body type?)

8. What was starting your first period like?

9. How did you feel about yourself as a teenager and young woman?

 10. Are you glad you are a woman? Why, or why not?

11. What do you like best about yourself?

12. What do you enjoy the least about yourself?

13. How does or did your mother feel about being a woman? (If you don't know for certain, what's your best guess?)

Okay. We do want to honor our mothers, but that does not mean we ignore their failings. We honor them by truthfully acknowledging their impact on us. We live in a broken world where no woman has ever been or ever had a perfect mother.

14. Where were you missed by your mom? Failed? Hurt? (In utero? As an infant? As a child? As a teenager? As a young woman? As a grown woman? Today?)

Spend time in prayer over these things. You are worth tears. You are worth sacrificing for. You are worth all the love and attention of the God of the universe.

Pray through the prayers at the end of chapter 5 of *Becoming Myself*. Don't rush. Invite Jesus in and keep inviting him in. The prayers are rewritten here to help you. Make any notes you want. Take note of where it is easy to pray and where it is more difficult.

Holy Trinity, I invoke your healing presence now. Come and meet me here and now. I sanctify my memories and my imagination to you, God. I ask you to come and to reveal where I need healing, Jesus, and I ask you to heal me.

Where do you want to come, God? Where do I need you to come? Is it while I was in the womb? Is it as a child, a little girl, a young woman? Is it to every stage of my life?

Come, Jesus. I ask you to come for me and to heal me in the deep places and unseen realms of my heart. I need you. Come with your light and your love, come with your tender, strong, and merciful Presence and fill me here.

In the Name of Jesus, I bless my conception. God, you planned on me before the earth was made. I bless my development in my mother's womb. God, you were there. Come now beyond the bounds of time and minister to me, your precious one, as I was being formed in my inmost being, and speak your love and delight over me. I confess to you, God, and proclaim the truth that I have all I need. I am fully satisfied in you, Jesus, and I always will be. I am wanted, delighted in, and of immeasurable worth. You planned on me. You wanted me, and you still want me. Like a weaned child within me, my soul is satisfied in you, God.

I break off any and all curses assigned to me, including all judgments against me passed on from my generational line. I am adopted into your family. The very blood of Jesus has purchased me, and I belong to you forever as your daughter. I claim this right here, in the womb.

Together with you, Jesus, I bless my delivery. Come into that time and space, dear Jesus. Come into any and all trauma or fear that I may have experienced in that. I break off all assignments of fear or death that may have entered in through a traumatic birth in the Name of Jesus Christ.

Jesus, my healer, come into my need for nurture; come into the places that needed nurture from my mother. Show me where healing is needed here.

Jesus, my healer, come into my need for protection; come into the places that needed protection offered to me by my mother. Show me where healing is needed here.

Jesus, my healer, come into my need for preparation; come into the places that needed preparation from my mother. Show me where healing is needed here.

Finally, Father God, in this moment I also repent of any and all hatred of women that has taken root in my heart. Hatred of women is hatred of myself and not from you. I choose to love women, and I embrace my own womanhood. I thank you that I am a woman! I bless my femininity! I thank you for my life, and I choose life. I give my life fully to you now, Jesus, and I invite you to have your way in me. I love you, Jesus. Thank you for coming for me; keep coming for me. I pray all of this in your glorious and beautiful Name, Jesus Christ. Amen.

Okay. That was good. Don't rush from this place. Let these prayers settle into your heart before you move on. And keep coming back to them. Continue to press into Jesus and ask for more and deeper healing as he prompts you to do so.

15. Initiating a daughter into womanhood and separating from her are two very difficult tasks. Has your mother blessed your coming into your own life? For good or ill, how is that affecting you?

16. If your mother could write you a letter expressing all you would love for her to say, what would it say? Take time right now, and pray, asking God to guide you. Then write the letter yourself.

Dearest Daughter,

17. And if you were free to write to your mother what you would truly like to say, what would you say? Take the time to say it now. (This is for you to write, not to send. Perhaps you will give a letter to your mother someday, but for this exercise, don't edit yourself.)

Dear Mom,

I just have to pause here and say, "Well done!" That can be a tough exercise, but it is such a good one to have done!

I love the following scripture. I take it as a promise.

> But I have calmed and quieted my soul,
>   like a weaned child with its mother;
>   like a weaned child is my soul within me.
>   (Ps. 131:2 ESV)

There is hope for us. There is healing. Nothing is out of reach for Jesus. *Weaned* means satisfied. *I am satisfied. I have had enough. All is well.* A weaned child is a satisfied child. Full. Content. Has enough. We can know that. We can. Dear hearts, we *can* be satisfied. God put us in a world where we have him and we have one another.

A woman once told me that there are all kinds of ways God brings daughters into our lives, and I have found that to be true. Well, it is also true that there are all kinds of ways God brings us mothers, too. Spiritual mothers. Friends. Counselors. Christ himself.

 18. Has God brought other mothers into your life? Who are they, and how are they mothering you?

Close your time today by thanking God and blessing these women. If you don't have women you can say are mothering you these days, ask God to bring them. And as always, let God continue to mother you, to heal you. Stay with this. Continue to pray and press in toward the more that God has for you.

Suggested Music: "I Am" by Jill Phillips; "Healer" by Hillsong

Suggested DVDs: *The Help, Tangled*

from accepting to embracing/ from fear to desire

Before you begin responding to the questions in this session, please read chapters 6 and 7 in the book *Becoming Myself.*

Spanx, schmanx. Girdles, schmirdles. I'm glad that I'm a woman, but I admit I continue to struggle with some aspects of my body. I know I'm not alone in that and that most women have things about their appearance they would like to change. Those with curly hair prefer straight and vice versa. (I just gave out a really big sigh.)

The thing is, God created you *you*. He created your body, your hair, your feet. And God does all things well. You are a lovely creation. (And yes, so am I!) Your body is a gift through which you experience his grace in every form of living.

Making peace with our bodies will lead to a great good. Go ahead and wear sandals in the summer! Sleeveless dresses are for all of us! Although making peace can take some time—particularly if your life has been thick with not liking your body so much—it is worth pursuing. God made your body. He loves it. He wants you to love it, care for it, and bless it too!

Dear Jesus, please help me with the study this week and with this topic for the rest of my life. You know what I like about how you made me and the things I don't care for. Would you please help me to see my body the way you do and be grateful for it? Would you please help me to believe that what you say about me is true? I am a beautiful woman! Today. Holy Spirit, guide me and fill me. I consecrate every part of my life to you. I love you. I need you. In Jesus's Name, I pray. Amen.

 1. Thank God for your body. Be specific. Bless all of your parts, even the jiggly bits. Write your blessing here.

Right now, God is saying this about you:

> How beautiful you are, my darling!
>> Oh, how beautiful!
> Your eyes behind your veil are doves. (Song 4:1)

God not only accepts us, he embraces us. Body and soul. He made our unique personalities just as he crafted our unique forms. Embracing ourselves is a stretch for most of us, but consider: Jesus commands us to love our neighbor as we love ourselves. How can we love our neighbor as ourselves if we do not love ourselves? How can we become joyful women if we are unable to see the humor in our own folly? We do become even more ourselves as we repent of areas in our lives that have nothing to do with faith or love, but God does not live in a perpetual state of disappointment over who we are. He enjoys us! Berating ourselves for our flaws and weaknesses only serves to undermine our strength to become.

Repenting from our sin is essential.

Beating ourselves up for sinning is no longer an option.

 2. Is there anything that Jesus is asking you to repent of? Ask him, and sit with the question for a few minutes. This isn't a scavenger hunt, just a time to humble yourself before him. If he raises something, then repent. Give it to God. Ask for his forgiveness. Receive it. Ask him here to help you to change and then thank him with faith for doing just that.

Our hope doesn't rest on our finally getting it together. Our hope rests in Jesus. And Jesus has proven once and for all, beyond a shadow of a doubt, that he loves us. The center of his heart is fiery devotion, love, commitment, and a passionate pursuit of *y-o-u*. He not only loves you, he likes you. You get to like you too. Which includes no longer shunning yourself but embracing yourself.

Embracing ourselves has nothing to do with arrogance or settling for a lower version of who we are. Embracing ourselves has everything to do with embracing the goodness of God's creative work in us. It means trusting God, believing that all he has made is glorious and good. And that includes us. You are the only one who can be you. Let's explore unique *you*.

3. What do you enjoy? What do *you* like?

4. What do you *want*? Invite Jesus into your wanting.

It's okay to want, and it's okay to want *more*. Wanting more has nothing to do with being unsatisfied or lacking in your present reality. It's being open to the more that God wants to bring you in your own life. The possibilities for you are limitless! They are. Yes, they are. Maybe not for tomorrow but for your *life*.

 5. If you could do anything, anything at all, and be fantastic at it, what would it be?

We live in a dangerous world. We all know that. The suffering in the world is enough to break your heart on any given day. But those who belong to God have been promised many things, and all of them are good. One thing is promised in Jeremiah 29:11. Look it up!

 6. What has God promised you?

The other day, I was having a relaxing moment just staring into space when the thought went through my head unbidden: "What do I want?" The answer came quickly, without hesitation, "To not be afraid." I was surprised. Now I'm surprised that I was surprised! Hah! I invited Jesus into my desire to not be afraid and then began to journal the answer to this question: "What am I afraid of?" I invite you to do the same.

 7. What are you afraid of? (If nothing comes to mind, here's a prompt: What are you afraid of losing? What are you afraid of never having?)

Some of our fears are valid. Certainly, most of them are founded in reality. Of course, some are not. But either way, God does not want us to live in fear. Read 2 Timothy 1:7.

8. God has not given us a spirit of fear. What has he given us a spirit of?

The truth is that as believers we are daughters of the King and we have nothing to fear. Not for ourselves and not for those we love. Let's let our hearts rest in that truth for a moment.

9. Read 1 Corinthians 15:54. What has happened to death? How is that relevant to your fears?

10. Read Deuteronomy 31:6 and Hebrews 13:5. What is true? How is that relevant to your fears?

11. Read Proverbs 29:25. Where has the fear of people gotten you into trouble?

12. Read Matthew 10:28. Why should we not be afraid of people or of what they can do?

13. Okay, now read John 3:15, 36 and 1 John 5:12. Do you believe that Jesus is the Son of God? Have you received his life in exchange for yours? Have you asked him to forgive you your sins and surrendered

your life to him as your King and your Savior? (If not, do it now! There's a sample prayer at the end of the book *Becoming Myself*.) If the answer is "Yes!" what does your future hold? Write your thoughts here.

 14. Okay. You are forever surrounded by love and continually safe in the hands of God. He promises never to leave or forsake you. He says that your name is inscribed into his hands and that nothing can take you out. From that forever safe place, pray and ask God what his dreams are for you.

Beloved Jesus, I invite you deeply into my heart and ask you to awaken in me the dreams you have for me and for my life. Help me now, Lord, to dream with you and write it down. Thank you!

 15. Dream big. Dream wide. Write down your dreams and desires. Don't edit yourself! Nothing is too large, too outlandish, or too little to write down. (If you are meeting in a small group, share some of your dreams and desires with each other.)

more to think about

It can be very helpful to have a physical and visual representation of the holy, uneven exchange of Life for death. Taking Communion can be just that. You can do this by yourself, at church, or in your small group.

Share Communion. Prepare your heart for Communion, and imagine holding what you are most afraid of and bring that fear to Jesus. As you take Communion, imagine laying that fear at the feet of Jesus and picking up his love in its place.

Something else I've done with a group of women is use tea lights. Each woman lights her candle, which represents her fear(s), and when she is ready she brings it to the front where Communion is available. She offers to Jesus her fear(s) and receives his grace and love in return.

- In your journal, begin to make a list of what you are like—your personality, taste, and penchants. Next to those characteristics, write down why those characteristics are *good*.

Suggested Music: "Dreamer" by Bethany Dillon; "Awakening" by Hillsong United

Suggested DVD: *Dreamer: Inspired by a True Story*

the company of women/ beauty forged in suffering

Before you begin responding to the questions in this session,
please read chapters 8 and 9 in the book *Becoming Myself*.

I am not a cynic. Not really. Well, many mornings I do wake up cynical, but after I have invited the Holy Spirit to fill my heart and my mind, I'm not. Still, it wasn't a difficult decision to group the two chapters "The Company of Women" and "Beauty Forged in Suffering" together. So much of the quality of our inner life is shaped through suffering, and so much suffering comes to us through our relationships.

When we love and care for someone or something, the potential for suffering is inherent. The choice is given to us many times a day to continue to care and love or to seal off sections of our hearts and shut down. God is always calling us both to love and to stay open to our own hearts—where he lives in us. Isolation, fear, anger, and self-justification do not lead us to the life Jesus wants for us. With wisdom, we must choose Love. Always.

Let's pray.

Dear Jesus, please help me with these chapters. Please open my eyes to your heart for me and all that you want to reveal to me. I long to become the woman I am meant to be. Help me to be honest with these topics—including the places where I have been or am now so deeply hurt. Please come into the relationships with women that I cherish as well as the ones I ache over or long for. Revive my heart. Revive my hope. Hold me close and help me to understand and receive what you long to reveal to me. In Jesus's Name, I pray. Amen.

1. Who are the women in your life? (A mom, sisters, coworkers, neighbors, friends?) In what capacities are you engaging with other women?

2. What are your friendships like? (Satisfying, enriching, disappointing, terrifying?) How often do you talk with or get together with women friends?

 3. When have you been hurt by women friends? How old were you? What happened?

4. How have those experiences shaped your current relationships?

forgive

We are human beings, so we are bound to fail one another. Further, we get our feelings hurt by other people who willfully or unintentionally wound us. Either way, Jesus commands us to forgive them and to come out of the trap of harboring an offense.

 5. Who do you need to forgive now? (Maybe it's yourself.) Ask Jesus to help you forgive those offenses. Go ahead now and pray. Really. (Some places are so tender and wounded that it may take a while for us to feel like we have forgiven a person. It's okay to simply pray again should the negative feelings or memories resurface.)

6. What would you love to share or experience with women friends?

7. When have you failed women in your life? What did you learn about yourself? How have those events shaped you in your current relationships?

soul ties

 8. The category of unhealthy "soul ties" is new to many women, but once described it is rarely an unfamiliar one. Galatians 6:14 declares that through the cross of Christ "the world has been crucified to me, and I to the world." The cross changes every relationship. Even family ties. Do you have personal experience with unhealthy "soul ties"?

The only bond we are urged to maintain is the bond of love by the Holy Spirit. All others—well, it's time to break them. You won't believe how free you can be and how good you can feel!

It is very important to note that breaking a soul tie with a person is not the same thing as *rejecting* the person. It is actually the *loving* thing to do. You don't want them obsessing about you, and you don't want to be obsessing about them. You don't want them controlling you, and you don't want to be controlling them. You don't want any further conversations with them when they aren't even there, and you don't want them doing this with you. You certainly don't want their warfare, and they don't want yours.

This simple prayer will help. Take the time right now to pray it!

By the cross of Jesus Christ I now sever all soul ties with [name her] in the Name of Jesus Christ. I am crucified to her, and she is crucified to me. I bring the cross of Christ between us, and I bring the love of Christ between us. I send [name her]'s spirit back to her body, and I forbid her warfare to transfer to me or to my domain. I command my spirit back into the Spirit of Jesus Christ in my body. I release [name her] to you, Jesus. I entrust her to you. Bless her, God, in your deep love! In Jesus's Name. Amen.

treasure the gift

9. Friends are a gift to us—to be nurtured and valued. Think a few minutes now about the friends God has entrusted to you. How can you offer love to them? (It may be as simple as a message saying you are thinking of them!)

 10. Is the thought that Jesus would love to be your closest friend a new one to you? Whether it is or it isn't, spend some time now and ask him to become that.

suffering

Since you are alive, I know you have suffered much and are to some level suffering even today. This is not an invitation to wallow in self-pity but to honor our own story and the work of our God in our lives. Though God does not cause all suffering, he certainly allows it. He not only allows it; he uses suffering to hone us and shape us.

 11. Thinking back on your life, what have been a few of the most difficult seasons for you? Take your time here. Really.

 12. What did you come to believe about God in and through those painful trials?

13. What did you come to believe about yourself?

14. Were those conclusions true? Really?

15. What difficulty are you facing or living with now?

16. Look up Romans 8:28. Looking back on your life, how might this be true concerning what you have suffered?

17. Who do you know who has suffered intensely in their life? What have they done with it?

We can choose to let suffering soften us or harden us. We can choose whether we will allow it to make us more compassionate or let our hearts become jealous of others. We can choose whether we will love Jesus in it or resent him for it. Only one set of choices will make us more beautiful.

 18. What would you love to be the fruit of the suffering you are currently enduring or have endured in the past?

19. Pray and ask God for that fruit. Ask him here to reveal places in your heart that need his tending and loving truth. Thank him that he promises to work all things—even the painful things—for your good.

20. Read Isaiah 61:3. Now ask Jesus to do what he is so very good at doing.

Jesus, heal my broken heart, release me from all darkness. Comfort me in my suffering. Cleanse me from all evil that has gotten in or taken root in the places of my sorrow. Please give me a crown of beauty instead of ashes; make me beautiful here, Lord, in this. Give me the oil of gladness instead of mourning; lift my grief and sorrow and give me the oil of your gladness; give me a garment of praise instead of a spirit of despair. Rescue me, I pray. Thank you that you have and that you are Jesus. It's in your strong Name that I pray. Amen.

May his grace hold you with even more tenderness as you go into your day now.

Suggested Music: "Bridge over Troubled Water" by Simon and Garfunkel
Suggested DVD: *Seabiscuit*

stumbling into freedom

Before you begin responding to the questions in this session,
please read chapter 10 in the book *Becoming Myself.*

Many years ago on a family vacation, my youngest son and I participated in a
Dolphin Quest adventure. We were in a large tank with a few dolphins, and
at the appointed time we had our picture taken next to the amazing mammal.
We were even able to briefly touch its smooth, rubbery skin. It was fabulous.

Dolphins make me happy. When you see them zipping through the
water, they look utterly delighted, as if they are the keepers of a joyous secret
they would be only too happy to share.

This year, I received the gift of swimming in the ocean while surrounded by
a pod of dolphins. Not three or five. Not in a tank. But twenty, thirty, fifty dolphins swimming in the wide blue Pacific. Not trained to perform, the dolphins
were singing, gliding, and then leaping through the air with joy! They were
spinner dolphins in family groups—mommies with their babies—and their
beauty left me speechless. I am filled with holy wonder at the memory of it.

The first experience was amazing. The second experience was transcen-
dent. Actually it was a taste of heaven when all things will be restored. (In
heaven, please join me while I ride a winged horse, a beautiful lion, or perhaps
a humpback whale!) The dolphins in the tank were glorious. The dolphins
swimming freely were even more so. Being free is better. Always.

"It is for freedom that Christ has set us free" (Gal. 5:1).

Let's begin with prayer:

Lord Jesus, I consecrate myself to you, this day to you, and this study to you. I pray for your guidance and your help. Please fill this time. Quicken my heart and my mind in response to the nudges of your Spirit. I give you permission to take me wherever you want me to go. I am yours. Thank you that you have come to set me free. I pray to become increasingly free in your truth and love! In your Name. Amen.

1. What was your reaction to the story of "Daniel" in *Becoming Myself*? What struck you?

 2. Regarding personal freedom, do you feel you are as free as you would like to be?

freedom from sin

Because of what Jesus has accomplished for us through his death, his resurrection, and his ascension, we can be so very free. It all begins here—with an internal choice to let Christ so invade our hearts that we cannot be held by any sort of bondage internally. We choose to love, to forgive; we choose not to fear; we choose life.

Could it be any clearer? Our old way of life was nailed to the cross with Christ, a decisive end to that sin-miserable life—no longer at sin's every beck and call! ...

From now on, think of it this way: Sin speaks a dead language that means nothing to you; God speaks your mother tongue, and you hang on every word. You are dead to sin and alive to God. That's what Jesus did....

A new power is in operation. The Spirit of life in Christ, like a strong wind, has magnificently cleared the air, freeing you from a fated lifetime of brutal tyranny at the hands of sin and death. (Rom. 6:6, 11; 8:2 MSG)

 3. We are no longer slaves to sin. What recurrent sin(s) do you need to repent of and be free from the power of? Pray now.

 4. What else would you like to be free from? (Think about freedom from bondage and slavery. Freedom from other people's judgments. Freedom from making judgments of other people.)

5. Take some time right now and ask God to do that in you. He has come to set us free. He's not only great at it, he loves to do it increasingly throughout our lives.

6. What would you like to be free to *do*? Write it down!

7. Ask God here to bring you the freedom you long for.

To live in the freedom that Christ has for us, we need to obey him in every area of our life. In Matthew 7:1–2 Jesus says, "Do not judge, or you too will be judged. For in the same way you judge others, you will be judged, and with the measure you use, it will be measured to you."

 8. Are you aware of judging others currently? If you are, take time now and write out a blessing on them instead.

spiritual warfare

Spiritual warfare is designed to separate us from the love of God. Its goal is to keep us from living in the freedom that Jesus has purchased for us. Satan whispers to us when we have failed or sinned (or simply feel horrid) that we are nothing and no one. He is a liar. The fight for our freedom involves exposing the Devil for who he is even when his lies feel completely true. The battle is waged and won in our thought life: in our minds and in our *hearts.*

What we think about ourselves, others, or a circumstance informs how we perceive it, which informs the way we experience it. Our thoughts play out in our lives.

 9. What are you thinking about yourself, others, or your circumstances today? Yes, now! Do your thoughts align with the Word of God? How, or how not? (It's so important that they do. Because, dear one, our good fight of faith is to believe and stand in the truth for ourselves so that we might love God and others.)

10. So again, what's true? Read Colossians 3:12. What are you?

11. Read Ephesians 1:1–11. What has God done for you?

12. Read Jeremiah 31:3. With what kind of love does God love you?

Jesus has won our freedom in a spiritual showdown with Satan. But our Enemy still refuses to go down without a fight. He knows he cannot take down Jesus, the Victorious One. But Satan can still wound Jesus's heart by wounding ours. Jesus has won our freedom. But we need to receive it, claim it, and stand in it. That is our good fight of faith: believing that God is who he says he is and believing that we are who he says we are in the face of evidence surrounding us that screams the opposite.

 13. Below is a personal form of the prayer found in chapter 10. Thoughtfully pray this prayer out loud now. Take your time with it. The fruit of it is really good.

Praise you, Jesus. Thank you for all you have accomplished for me. I love you. I worship you. You are the King of kings and Lord of lords, and your Name is above every other name that can be given in this age or in the age to come. I come under your authority now. I receive all the work that you accomplished for me by your cross and death, by your resurrection, and by your ascension. I take my place in your authority now, and in your Name, Jesus, I come against every foul spirit that has been harassing me. I bring the cross and blood of Jesus Christ against every foul spirit of [what has been attacking you? Hatred, rage, intimidation, shame, accusation judgment, offense, misunderstanding, fear, panic, dread, hopelessness, despair?] *I bring your blood and cross against these foul spirits. In the Name of Jesus Christ and by your authority I command every foul spirit bound to the throne of Jesus Christ for judgment. I break every agreement I have made with the Enemy, and I renounce them now. I make my agreement with the Truth.*

Father, please send your angels to enforce this command. Thank you, God. Praise you. I worship you, Jesus. I long to be free, to know you and to love you more deeply and truly. You are worthy. Please remove everything that separates me from knowing you as you truly are and keeps me from living in the freedom that you have purchased for me. In Jesus's mighty Name. Amen.

We demolish arguments and every pretension that sets itself up against the knowledge of God, and we take captive every thought to make it obedient to Christ. (2 Cor. 10:5)

I have a handwritten sign on my desk. It says:

> **God has given me his AUTHORITY.** *I need to use it.*
> *Feel:*   *Disqualified?*
>   *Lonely?*
>   *Like a failure?*
>   *A disappointment?*
>   *Hopeless?*
>   *Overwhelmed?*
>   *Depressed?*
>   *Discouraged?*
>   *Like giving up?*
>   *Unloved?*
>   *Unwanted?*
>   *Un ...?*
> **It's warfare. Submit. Resist. Stand. Fight.**

I can't tell you how helpful it has been. (You can make your own if you want! Put it on your desk. Tape it to your mirror!) When negative but familiar thoughts and feelings come upon me, I want to be quick to recognize them as lies from the pit of hell. Too often, they feel so true that I swallow them and spiral down. When I engage my will and my spirit and bring my heart before God in prayer—submitting to his authority and resisting the lies of the Enemy—the heaviness lifts. It is vitally important that we are aware of what we are thinking, believing, feeling, and accepting as true.

14. So again. What are you thinking right now? About this topic? About God? About you?

15. Are your thoughts in agreement with the Word of God? If they are, great! If they're not—lay them down and pick up the truth.

Jesus has freedom for us, sisters. And it is found when we align ourselves with the heart of our God. It takes practice. It is worth it!

Suggested Music: "I Am Set Free" by All Sons and Daughters; "Great I Am" by Jared Anderson

becoming a woman of faith and worship

Before you begin responding to the questions in this session, please read chapters 11 and 12 in the book *Becoming Myself*.

I love these three inspiring women: Mary the mother of Jesus, Mary of Bethany, and Mary Magdalene. Each of these Marys is a heroine of the faith, and these two chapters could easily be a book unto themselves. This week, let's ask God to reveal what he would have us learn from these women.

Let's pray.

Dear God, thank you for choosing me to be yours before you even made the world. I am yours. I pray right now to be open to what you would have me learn from these women who loved you so passionately. I want to be a woman of faith, love, and extravagant worship. I want to follow you closely, trust you fully, and know you intimately. Please reveal your heart more deeply to me this day. I consecrate my life to you. Come, Holy Spirit, and guide me. Fill this time. Fill me. Thank you! In Jesus's Name, I pray. Amen.

1. We will focus on the three Marys from the New Testament: Mary the mother of Jesus, Mary of Bethany, and Mary Magdalene. Do you have a favorite? If you do, which one?

Mary the mother of Jesus

 2. What do you like about Mary, Jesus's mother?

 3. What do you think Simeon meant when he told Mary, "And a sword will pierce your own soul" (Luke 2:35)?

4. Has a sword pierced your soul? If so, what happened?

5. What do you think Jesus's tone was to his mother at the wedding in Cana (John 2) when he said, "Woman, why do you involve me? ... My hour has not yet come" (v. 4)?

> Mary treasured up all these things and pondered them in
> her heart. (Luke 2:19)

I love that Mary treasured "all these things" in her heart. She was familiar with the prophecies. Mary actively remembered. Late at night, while nursing her little baby, she would pull out these treasures and think on them. She was a woman of wisdom who knew what to store in her heart, what to treasure, what to ponder.

6. It's a good thing to ask ourselves: what are we pondering? When you can't sleep at night, where do your thoughts tend to go?

 7. What would you like to actively remember?

8. Regarding Jesus, Mary is telling each of us to "do whatever he tells you" (John 2:5). What does that mean to you today?

Mary of Bethany

 9. What do you like about Mary of Bethany?

10. It is very easy in our busy world to exchange relationship with Jesus for service of him. We can all relate to Mary's sister, Martha, quite well. What is the first and greatest commandment?

 11. What might loving Jesus look like for you today?

We know from the Bible that Jesus loved Lazarus, yet he did not run to his aid when Lazarus was sick unto death. Mary and Martha longed for Jesus to come—they had sent word and asked for him to come—but he didn't. At least not in the timing they had hoped for. They had to wait. Waiting for God is one of the hardest things we ever have to do, isn't it?

 12. What are you asking Jesus to do? What are you waiting for?

Believing God is good in the midst of waiting is incredibly hard. Believing God is good in the midst of immense sorrow, loss, or pain is even more difficult. Those are the times when our faith, the treasure of our hearts, is tested by fire and becomes gold. What we come to know of God—and the terrain he comes to inhabit in our hearts through the trial—leads people to say, "I wouldn't change a thing." That's the crazy, supernatural realm of God.

I know there have been many times when God didn't answer your prayers in the way you wanted or in the timing you wanted. But what he did in the end was far better. Even if the "far better" was your coming to depend on him more deeply through the travail.

13. Do you have a story of a time when God did not come in the way or the timing that you had wanted but what unfolded was even better than you had hoped for? What happened?

14. Regarding what you are asking God for these days, spend a few minutes in prayer. Ask your Father here to answer your prayer in the way you long for, or to do something even better.

15. Mary of Bethany anointed Jesus with oil and was rebuked by the disciples for it. They misunderstood and judged her. Have you been misunderstood or judged by others for doing what you thought was right? What happened?

16. What does it feel like to know that Jesus never misunderstands you? He completely "gets" you.

 17. Mary poured out her offering of love and worship to Jesus via her life savings of precious nard. She loved him recklessly. What might it look like for you to offer Jesus your worship recklessly? What would you like to pour out on Jesus?

Mary Magdalene

 18. What stirs you about Mary Magdalene?

19. Where was she when Jesus was crucified? What does that say about her?

 20. Imagine yourself back in time. Where do you think you would have been when Jesus was being crucified? Where would you like to have been?

21. Why do you think Jesus appeared to Mary Magdalene first after his resurrection?

22. Have you ever been chosen? Set apart? When? How'd it feel?

 23. Whether you can remember a time of being chosen or not, you have been chosen in the very best of ways! Look up these verses and underline them in your own Bible.

You did not choose me, but I chose you. (John 15:16)

For he chose us in him before the creation of the world. (Eph. 1:4)

God's chosen people, holy and dearly loved. (Col. 3:12)

 24. What are some things that happen when we worship Jesus?

In our loving of Jesus we become increasingly available for him to continue his deep work in us, transforming us into the women we long to be.

Worshipping Jesus enables us to be like Mary of Bethany and to minister to him with our adoration, our tears, and our thankful hearts. Why don't you take a few minutes and come before him now? Imagine you are sitting at his feet and listening, or washing his feet with your tears, or gazing up at him on the cross, or even bowing before the very much alive and risen Lord. There is no doing this wrong. It makes God so happy when we pause in the midst of our day or create an extended time alone with him, simply to adore him!

Jesus, I come to you with all that I am. I give you my love and my thanks. Thank you for choosing me! Thank you for dying for me! Thank you that you rose from the dead and are seated at the right hand of God. Thank you for your faithfulness, strength, and love. I worship you, Jesus. I give you all that I am. I offer you my desire, my gifting, my weakness, my need, my failure, my hope—my everything. I worship you with all that I am and all that I have and even all that I am not. You are worthy of all praise and honor. I love you. I pray to love you even more! Dearest Jesus, please reveal yourself to me as you truly are. Even now. In your Name, I pray. Amen.

more to think about

Have a time of intimate worship. Remember, intimate worship is simply telling God how wonderful he is and why. It is pouring out our love onto him like oil. We bring him all that we are as women, even our weariness and sorrow. Take twenty to thirty minutes, play anointed worship music in the background, and practice coming before Jesus just to love on him. He will love it!

Suggested Music: "The More I Seek You" by Klaus Kuehn; "Beloved" by Sarah Reeves; "Undivided Focus" by Heather Clark; "Come to Me" by Bethel Music, featuring Jenn Johnson; "More than Ashes" by Tim Reimherr/Merchant Band; "Who Can Compare" by Emerging Voices/Jesus Culture

becoming our true name/take heart

Before you begin responding to the questions in this session, please read chapters 13 and 14 in the book *Becoming Myself.*

I went to a banquet recently with my husband, and the tables were set with lots of spoons, several forks, many glasses, and at the top of each place setting—a piece of pie. Soon after sitting down, John said with a smile, "I'm a grown-up now, and I don't have to wait!" and took a bite of his dessert.

I have always liked the T-shirt that says, "Eat Dessert First." Sometimes, like that rare moment for my non-dessert-loving husband, I don't want to "save the best for last." I want it first! But then again, sometimes I do like saving the best for last. That's how I feel about these chapters.

Let's begin our last session with prayer!

Dear Jesus,
I come under your authority.
I come under your love.
I give myself to you utterly.

I lay down everything that I've been carrying and give myself to you: my heart, mind, soul, body, and spirit—everything in me.
Please cleanse me afresh with your blood.
I ask your Spirit to restore my union with you!
Fill me with your Life! Give me eyes to see and ears to hear you.
Remove everything that is in between you and me, Jesus. I love you.
It's in your mighty Name that I pray. Amen.

Our belief about our true identity lays the foundation for every aspect of our lives. What we believe about ourselves plays out with our every breath. The answer to the question, "Who do you think you are?" is fundamental.

1. So, who do you think you are?

2. Do you have a nickname? What names (good or bad) were you called while you were growing up?

 3. What names do you call yourself? When you pass a mirror? When you blow it?

4. What's your given name? What does it mean?

Shakespeare famously wrote in *Romeo and Juliet*, "What's in a name? … A rose by any other name would smell as sweet." After giving it much thought, I have to admit that I think Shakespeare got this bit wrong. A rose by any other name would not smell as sweet. The power of what we call something affects our experience of it. Dramatically.

 5. What does God call a believer in his Word? (Recall some things from chapter 13 of the book.)

6. What would it be like right now to entertain the possibility in your heart that all God says about you is true? Let your heart go there for a few minutes.

    You are his delight.

    You make him happy just by being you.

    He thinks you're lovely.

    You are his beloved.

    You are the one who has captured his heart.

7. Remember the scoreboard story? About what does your enemy "talk smack" to you?

 8. Who are you? *Really?* Put some words to yourself.

You are a child of God.

Jesus has won our victory, and we are victorious as well, in him. We are not defined by our sin, our failures, or our past. We are forever and only defined by the finished work of Jesus Christ. Everything Jesus did and won was for us. We were slaves to sin, yes. But because of Jesus, we are slaves no longer. We are daughters. We are brides.

> *Watch your thoughts, for they become words. Watch your words,*
> *for they become actions. Watch your actions, for they become*
> *habits. Watch your habits, for they become your character.*
> *And watch your character, for it becomes your destiny!*
> —Author Unknown

What we think, we become.

 9. This is so vitally important, and it has to be personal. We need to know who *we* are to God. So then, we must ask him. Ask God. Right now. *Am I your beloved? How do you see me? Do you delight in*

me? Do you love me because you're God and that's your job, or do you love me simply for me?

10. You, dear heart, you *are* the Beloved. God will ask you to risk many things. But perhaps the most difficult risk is the risk of faith. You must risk *believing*.

Pray this:

Jesus, I choose to believe I am your Beloved and your desire is for me. I choose to believe I am no longer forsaken or deserted, but I am your Delight, sought after and dearly loved. Jesus, I want to become the woman you have in mind for me. Show me who she is; show me who I really am, who I was always meant to be. Tell me my true name; give me an image of who you see me becoming. Give me eyes to see and ears to hear and the courage to accept what you are saying. Tell me, Jesus.

11. Ask Jesus, *Do you have a special name for me?* (When he tells you, dear one, choose to believe.)

> You will be called by a new name
> that the mouth of the LORD will bestow. (Isa. 62:2)

12. While we are talking about naming things, let's take a few moments and name our lives. We want to name them blessed and good. Take a few minutes

now and do that. Go ahead and ask God to reframe the way you think of your life and what is required of you. Begin this practice now. And it is a practice, gals. One that we will get better at over time—the more we practice it!

As long as we are risking things, it's time to take what is perhaps the biggest risk of all and ...

 13. Ask God to give you his vision of the woman you are to become. What's she like? Write out by faith the description of the woman you are becoming.
I am becoming a woman who is ...

Having a vision of who you are becoming informs your present. We live today knowing who we are going to be tomorrow. Own and embrace this woman, this higher version of yourself, this woman you are becoming.

14. What is God asking you to risk in order for you to become the woman you are called to be?

15. What does *confidence* mean? Where are we to place our confidence?

16. In Romans 8:5, Paul says, "But those who live in accordance with the Spirit have their minds set on what the Spirit desires." What does the Spirit desire? (Hints: Gal. 5:22; Phil. 4:8.)

17. Today, what are you thinking about? What has captured your attention? Remember, we move toward what we focus on. Our attention becomes our intention. What do you want to be moving toward?

> Let us [fix] our eyes on Jesus, the pioneer and perfecter of faith. (Heb. 12:1–2)

 18. What do you want to offer?

God made you *you* on purpose. *You are meant to offer the world the fullest expression of your unique self, crafted in a joint partnership between you and God.*

19. Read Galatians 2:20. Who lives in and through you?

20. Read Colossians 1:27. What is the mystery of our faith?

 21. Write a prayer of thanksgiving to God for making you *you*. Thank him in faith and trust for all that he has done and will do in and through your life.

It is utterly essential that in fixing our gaze on Jesus, we remember that he is our everything. He is the secret to our own becoming. He is the secret to living, enjoying, and offering life. He is the secret of our hope and our faith, and the love of our life.

22. Read Philippians 2:13. Just to be ever so clear, what is the secret to becoming your true self and living the life you long to live?

Jesus is the only one with the strength to pull off this life of ours. He has the capacity to navigate every season of our lives and every difficult situation we face. He has the wisdom to guide us, the faithfulness to encourage us, and the love to shield us. Because we are his followers, his Spirit lives within us. We are never alone on the journey of becoming, never left to our own devices to figure life out, and never abandoned along the way.

23. Our prayer, "Christ in us, live this day. Christ in us, love this person. Christ in us, [fill in the blank]" becomes our breath and he our daily bread. Pray that now.

His name is Faithful and True. He has dreams of you and for you. He has embraced you in fierce love, inscribed your true name into the palm of his hand, and pledged himself to you forever.

You are in good hands.

Your future is blessed.

Your name is lovely.

You are becoming ever more his. Which means, dearest, you are becoming yourself.

> *Be who God meant you to be and you will set the world on fire.*
> —St. Catherine of Siena

more to think about

In your small group, after spending these weeks together hearing one another's hearts, dreams, and visions of becoming, spend a few minutes taking turns speaking over each woman. One idea is simply to have each of the other women in the group offer an adjective that describes something good or enjoyable about one woman, and then move to the next woman. Another idea is to pray over each woman, blessing the journey she is on and agreeing with God over who she is becoming.

Suggested Music: "I Am New" by Jason Gray; "Homeward Bound" by Kristene Mueller; "Take Heart" by Hillsong United

parting words

I pray that this has been an enriching experience for you. The challenge that lies before each one of us now is the same. Jesus told us what it is when he spoke these words to Jairus, and he is speaking them to us today: "Don't be afraid; just believe" (Luke 8:50).

Believe the Word of God is true. It is true for you. Believe Jesus.

God also commands us to *remember*. Remember the good things God has done. Remember *who he is*. Remember *who you are* in Christ. Remember that it is God who works in you to will and to act in order to fulfill his good purpose (Phil. 2:13). And he is working all things together for your good.

I encourage you to not walk away from this study guide and simply leap into the next thing. Stay with the messages presented here. Linger with what God has stirred in your heart. Review your dreams list (session 4, question 15). Add to it! Continue to press into becoming a woman of faith and extravagant worship. Choose to engage your world by stepping more fully into the woman you truly are.

You are a glorious creation of the Lord Jesus Christ, and you were brought into this world for "such a time as this." We need you. And yet it isn't up to you. Take heart, dear one. You are loved beyond telling, and the greatest act of your life will be to respond to the heart of God simply by loving Jesus back. The way that love will express itself through your life is unique and priceless and beautiful. One day, at the Feast of the Lamb, we will get to hear the stories of each other's lives, and only heaven will be able to contain the joy.

I look forward to meeting you.

With hope and love—on the journey with you,
Stasi

notes for discussion leaders

A small group working through this material will benefit from having a discussion leader. If that's you, don't worry—you don't need to have all the answers. All you need is the willingness to prepare each week, guide the discussion, and rely on the Holy Spirit to work in your heart and the hearts of group members.

discussion leader's job description

Like I said before, the discussion leader's job isn't to have all the answers. She simply needs to:

- Keep the group on track when it's tempted to go off on a tangent.
- Keep the discussion moving so that it doesn't get stuck on one question.
- Make sure that everyone gets a chance to talk and that no one dominates. (It is not necessary that every person respond aloud to every question, but every person should have the chance to do so.)
- Make sure that the discussion remains respectful.

preparing for the discussion

As the discussion leader, you'll need to read the chapters from *Becoming Myself* before each session. If you're using the DVD and can view it ahead of time, that's great. Work through your own responses to the questions ahead of time as well.

In most sessions it won't be possible for your group to cover all of the questions in one ninety-minute discussion. So as you prepare, give some thought to selecting those questions your group will most benefit from discussing. To help you with that, I've used a leaf to highlight questions as suggested ones to be sure to cover. Some of the questions are instructions for prayer—you don't need to pray these together if group members are praying them at home.

Just before the meeting, be sure the chairs are arranged so that everyone can see each other's faces.

guiding the discussion

If you have a copy of the *Becoming Myself DVD*, view the session video right after you open the meeting with prayer. After the video, discuss the questions you have chosen. Feel free to read a section of text out loud if the group is unclear on what a question is getting at. Also, feel free to discuss just a few questions in your group meeting if the women are finding those questions especially helpful. You can take an extra meeting to cover the other questions or move on to the next session. Covering all the material is less important than encouraging spiritual growth.

A few ground rules can make the discussion deeper:

- *Confidentiality:* Whatever is said in the group stays in the group. Nothing is to be repeated to those who weren't there.
- *Honesty:* We're not here to impress each other. We're here to grow and to know each other.
- *Respect:* Disagreement is welcome. Disrespect is not.

The discussion should be a conversation among the group members, not a one-on-one with the leader. You can encourage this with statements like,

"Thanks, Allison! What do others of you think?" or "Does anyone have a similar experience, or a different one?"

Don't be afraid of silence—it means group members are thinking about how to answer a question. Trust that the Spirit is working in the members of your group, and wait. Sometimes it's helpful to rephrase the question in your own words. Then wait for others' responses, and avoid jumping in with your own.

Most of all, spend time praying for your group. You can't talk anyone into becoming her true self. Pray that the Spirit of God would fill your lives and do the impossible in and through you. May God accomplish the extraordinary in your lives as you seek to follow Jesus with everything you've got.

notes

1. "Misogyny," Merriam-Webster's Collegiate Dictionary, Eleventh Edition, s.v. "misogyny," www.merriam-webster.com/dictionary/misogyny (accessed May 31, 2012).

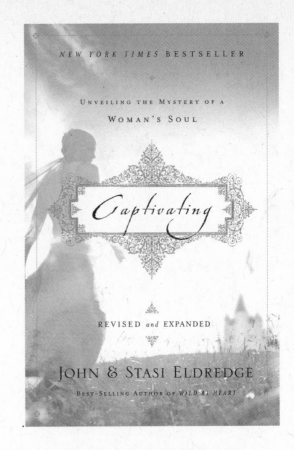

AVAILABLE
WHEREVER
BOOKS and EBOOKS
ARE SOLD

Every woman was once a little girl.
And every little girl holds in her heart
her most precious dreams.
She longs to be swept up into
a romance, to play an irreplaceable
role in a great adventure, to be
the beauty of the story. Those desires
are far more than child's play.
They are the secret to the feminine heart.

YOUR HEART MATTERS
MORE THAN ANYTHING ELSE
IN ALL CREATION.

Like Stasi

f join her on facebook!